PROFIT PULSE

Amplifying Wealth with Cutting-Edge Methods

Shah Rukh

CONTENTS

INTRODUCTION

In a rapidly changing world, achieving success in business requires more than just a focus on financial profitability. Today's organizations face the challenge of balancing profitability with ethical practices, sustainability, and social responsibility. The book "Sustainable Success: Balancing Profitability and Ethical Practices" explores the dynamic relationship between profitability and ethical considerations, providing insights into how organizations can create long-term value while addressing societal and environmental challenges.

The book takes a comprehensive approach to understanding the concept of sustainable success. It delves into the rise of sustainability as a business imperative, exploring the evolution of sustainability frameworks and the benefits of integrating sustainable practices into business strategies. It emphasizes the importance of ethical practices in building trust with stakeholders and highlights the role of corporate social responsibility (CSR) in driving positive social impact.

The first chapters of the book lay the foundation by explaining the concepts of sustainability, ethical practices, and the integration of these principles into business strategies. It examines the evolution of sustainability as a response to the changing expectations of consumers, investors, and society at large. By exploring frameworks such as the triple bottom line and the United Nations Sustainable Development Goals, readers gain a deeper understanding of how sustainability goes beyond financial considerations to encompass environmental and social dimensions.

The book then delves into the dynamics of ethical practices, exploring ethical frameworks and standards that guide organizations in making responsible decisions. It highlights the importance of ethical decision-making, transparency, and accountability in building trust and maintaining long-term relationships with stakeholders. Through examples of corporate scandals and ethical dilemmas, readers gain insights into the consequences of unethical practices and the need for organizations to prioritize ethical behavior.

Integrating sustainability into business strategies is a key focus of the book. It examines various strategies and approaches for incorporating sustainability considerations into core business practices. From sustainable supply chain management to responsible sourcing and product life cycle assessment, readers gain practical insights into how organizations can reduce their environmental footprint and promote sustainable practices throughout their operations.

The book also explores the concept of corporate social responsibility (CSR) and its role in driving positive social impact. It discusses the benefits of CSR initiatives such as philanthropy, employee volunteering, and community engagement. Through case studies and best practices, readers discover how organizations can align their values with the needs of society, making a meaningful difference while enhancing their reputation and stakeholder relationships.

Furthermore, the book addresses environmental sustainability and the importance of responsible environmental practices. It explores strategies for minimizing negative environmental impacts, reducing carbon emissions, and adopting renewable energy sources. By understanding the benefits of environmental sustainability, organizations can enhance their operational efficiency, comply with regulations, and contribute to a more sustainable future. The concept of social impact and stakeholder engagement is also examined in-depth. Readers gain insights into how organizations can generate positive social change by promoting diversity and inclusion, supporting local communities, and fostering ethical labor practices. Through effective stakeholder engagement, organizations can build sustainable relationships and create shared value for all stakeholders.

Ethical leadership and governance are essential components of sustainable success. The book emphasizes the importance of ethical leadership in setting the tone for ethical practices within organizations. It explores the role of governance structures, ethics codes, and whistleblower mechanisms in ensuring accountability and transparency. By understanding the significance of ethical leadership, readers gain insights into how organizations can foster an ethical culture and create an environment that supports sustainable success.

The book also addresses the concept of responsible investing, highlighting the growing demand for investments that integrate environmental, social, and governance (ESG) factors. It explores the role of ESG ratings and benchmarks in guiding responsible investment decisions and examines the potential financial benefits of incorporating sustainability considerations into investment strategies.

Lastly, the book emphasizes the importance of collaboration and partnerships for sustainable success. It explores the benefits of collective action, public-private partnerships, and industry coalitions in addressing complex social and environmental challenges. By fostering collaboration and embracing innovation, organizations can drive systemic change and create a more sustainable and equitable future.

In conclusion, "Sustainable Success: Balancing Profitability and Ethical Practices" provides a comprehensive guide to achieving long-term success by integrating ethical practices, sustainability, and social responsibility into business strategies. By understanding the dynamics of sustainable business practices and exploring practical examples and best practices, readers gain the knowledge and insights to create value, maintain stakeholder trust, and contribute to a better world.

CHAPTER 1: UNLEASHING THE PROFIT PULSE: EXPLORING CUTTING-EDGE METHODS

Introduction: In a rapidly evolving and highly competitive business landscape, staying ahead of the curve is crucial for amplifying wealth and achieving financial success. This chapter delves into the realm of cutting-edge methods that have the potential to revolutionize profit generation. By exploring these innovative approaches, individuals and businesses can unlock new avenues for growth, increase profitability, and gain a competitive edge.

1.1 The Need for Cutting-Edge Methods: The traditional methods of wealth creation are no longer sufficient in a world driven by technological advancements and disruptive innovations. This section highlights the need to embrace cutting-edge methods to adapt to changing market dynamics, seize emerging opportunities, and overcome challenges. It emphasizes the importance of continuously exploring and integrating new strategies to optimize financial outcomes.

1.2 Harnessing Technology for Profit Maximization: Technological advancements have transformed various industries and opened up unprecedented opportunities for profit amplification. This subsection explores how emerging technologies such as artificial intelligence, machine learning, automation, and big data analytics

1

can be leveraged to drive efficiency, enhance decision-making, and optimize business processes. It delves into case studies and real-world examples that demonstrate the transformative power of technology in amplifying wealth.

1.3 The Rise of Digital Assets: The advent of cryptocurrencies and blockchain technology has disrupted traditional notions of wealth creation and investment. This segment discusses the rise of digital assets, such as Bitcoin, Ethereum, and other cryptocurrencies, and their potential as cutting-edge methods for generating substantial profits. It explores the underlying technology, the benefits, and risks associated with digital assets, and provides insights on how to navigate this rapidly evolving landscape.

1.4 Innovations in Investment Strategies: Investment strategies have also witnessed a paradigm shift with the advent of cutting-edge methods. This section explores alternative investment vehicles, such as venture capital, private equity, hedge funds, and real estate syndication, which offer unique opportunities for high returns. It delves into the intricacies of these strategies, their risk-reward profiles, and provides guidance on how to capitalize on them effectively.

1.5 Embracing Disruptive Business Models: In a world characterized by disruption, businesses that fail to adapt risk being left behind. This subsection explores innovative business models, such as platform-based economies, sharing economies, and subscription-based services, that are reshaping industries and creating new avenues for profit generation. It highlights the success stories of companies that have harnessed cutting-edge business models and provides practical insights on how to adopt and implement them.

1.6 The Power of Data Analytics: Data has become the lifeblood of modern businesses, enabling organizations to gain deep insights, make informed decisions, and identify lucrative opportunities. This segment explores the field of data analytics, including predictive analytics, prescriptive analytics, and customer segmentation, and their role in amplifying wealth. It discusses the tools, techniques, and best practices for harnessing the power of data to optimize financial outcomes.

1.7 Mitigating Risks and Challenges: While cutting-edge methods offer immense potential for profit amplification, they also come with inherent risks and challenges. This section addresses the risks associated with new technologies, investment strategies, and disruptive business models. It provides strategies for risk management, highlights regulatory considerations, and emphasizes the importance of maintaining a balanced approach when exploring these methods.

1.8 Cultivating a Culture of Innovation: Successfully implementing cutting-edge methods requires a culture of innovation within individuals and organizations. This subsection explores the mindset, skills, and practices necessary to foster innovation and embrace change. It provides guidance on fostering creativity, encouraging experimentation, and cultivating a forward-thinking environment that encourages the exploration of new strategies.

Conclusion: Chapter 1 concludes by emphasizing the importance of exploring and adopting cutting-edge methods to amplify wealth. It underscores the need to embrace technology, innovation, and data-driven decision-making to stay ahead in an ever-evolving business landscape. By leveraging these cutting-edge methods, individuals and businesses can unlock new avenues for growth, optimize profitability, and thrive in the face of disruptive change.

CHAPTER 2: MAXIMIZING RETURNS: LEVERAGING ADVANCED INVESTMENT STRATEGIES

Introduction: Investing is a powerful tool for wealth creation, and the ability to maximize returns is a key objective for any investor. This chapter delves into advanced investment strategies that go beyond conventional approaches, aiming to optimize returns and capitalize on unique opportunities. By exploring these strategies, investors can gain insights into sophisticated techniques and principles that can significantly enhance their investment performance.

2.1 The Evolution of Investment Strategies: Investment strategies have evolved over time, driven by changes in market dynamics, advancements in technology, and the availability of new financial instruments. This section provides a historical overview of investment strategies, from traditional buy-and-hold approaches to the more advanced and dynamic methods employed today. It highlights the need for investors to adapt and embrace advanced strategies to maximize their returns in an increasingly complex investment landscape.

2.2 Active vs. Passive Investing: The debate between active and passive investing has gained significant attention in recent years. This subsection explores the characteristics, advantages, and limitations of both approaches. It discusses the role of active management in identifying mispriced assets and generating alpha, as well as the benefits of passive investing through low-cost index funds and ETFs. It also examines strategies that combine elements of both approaches, such as smart beta strategies and factor investing.

2.3 Alternative Investments: Traditional asset classes, such as stocks and bonds, are no longer the sole focus of investors seeking to maximize returns. This section explores alternative investments, including private equity, venture capital, hedge funds, real estate, commodities, and infrastructure. It examines the unique characteristics and potential benefits of these asset classes, as well as the challenges and risks involved. It also discusses strategies for accessing and incorporating alternative investments into an investment portfolio.

2.4 Risk Management and Portfolio Diversification: Maximizing returns involves striking a delicate balance between risk and reward. This subsection delves into risk management techniques and the importance of portfolio diversification. It discusses modern portfolio theory, asset allocation strategies, and the benefits of diversifying across different asset classes, geographic regions, and investment styles. It also explores the use of alternative risk measures, such as value at risk (VaR) and conditional value at risk (CVaR), to quantify and manage risk effectively.

2.5 Factor-Based Investing: Factor-based investing

has gained prominence as a systematic approach to generating superior risk-adjusted returns. This section explores factor investing, which involves targeting specific drivers of returns, such as value, momentum, size, quality, and low volatility. It discusses the academic research and empirical evidence supporting factor-based investing, as well as practical implementation considerations. It also examines multifactor strategies and smart beta products that offer exposure to multiple factors in a systematic manner.

2.6 Quantitative and Algorithmic Strategies: Advancements in computing power and data availability have revolutionized investment strategies. This subsection delves into quantitative and algorithmic strategies, where mathematical models and computer algorithms are employed to identify investment opportunities and execute trades. It discusses various quantitative approaches, such as statistical arbitrage, trend following, and mean reversion, as well as the role of high-frequency trading in today's markets. It also highlights the challenges and ethical considerations associated with algorithmic trading.

2.7 ESG and Sustainable Investing: Environmental, social, and governance (ESG) factors have gained prominence in investment decision-making. This section explores ESG and sustainable investing, which aim to generate both financial returns and positive societal impact. It examines the integration of ESG criteria into investment analysis and portfolio construction, as well as the growth of impact investing and thematic investing. It also discusses the measurement and reporting of ESG performance and the evolving regulatory landscape in this field.

2.8 Behavioral Finance and Investor Psychology: Understanding investor behavior and psychology is essential for maximizing returns. This subsection explores behavioral finance, which examines the biases, cognitive errors, and emotional factors that influence investment decisions. It discusses concepts such as loss aversion, overconfidence, herding behavior, and the disposition effect. It also provides insights into techniques for mitigating behavioral biases and improving investment decision-making.

Conclusion: Chapter 2 concludes by highlighting the importance of leveraging advanced investment strategies to maximize returns. It emphasizes the need for investors to adapt to changing market dynamics, embrace alternative investments, manage risks effectively, and leverage technological advancements. By incorporating these advanced strategies into their investment approach, investors can enhance their chances of achieving superior risk-adjusted returns and successfully navigate the complexities of the modern investment landscape.

CHAPTER 3: REVOLUTIONARY TECHNOLOGIES: DISRUPTING TRADITIONAL WEALTH CREATION

Introduction: Technological advancements have been the driving force behind significant disruptions in various industries, revolutionizing the way wealth is created and accumulated. This chapter explores the impact of revolutionary technologies on traditional wealth creation methods and examines how individuals and businesses can adapt to leverage these transformative forces. By understanding and embracing these technologies, readers can position themselves to take advantage of emerging opportunities and enhance their wealth creation strategies.

3.1 The Technological Revolution: The rapid advancement of technology has fundamentally altered the business landscape, challenging traditional models and creating new avenues for wealth creation. This section provides an overview of the technological revolution, highlighting the key technological drivers, such as artificial intelligence, robotics, internet of things, blockchain, and cloud computing. It emphasizes the need to adapt and embrace these technologies to stay competitive in today's dynamic environment.

3.2 Automation and Robotics: Automation and robotics

have significantly impacted industries, transforming production processes and optimizing operational efficiency. This subsection explores how automation and robotics technologies, such as industrial robots, process automation software, and machine learning algorithms, are disrupting traditional labor-intensive sectors. It discusses the benefits of automation, including increased productivity, cost savings, and improved quality control, while also addressing the potential impact on employment and the workforce.

3.3 Artificial Intelligence and Machine Learning: Artificial intelligence (AI) and machine learning (ML) have emerged as powerful tools for transforming data into valuable insights and driving informed decision-making. This section delves into the applications of AI and ML in various domains, including finance, healthcare, marketing, and supply chain management. It explores how AI and ML are automating tasks, enhancing predictive capabilities, and enabling personalized experiences, leading to improved efficiency and higher profitability.

3.4 Blockchain and Cryptocurrencies: Blockchain technology and cryptocurrencies have disrupted traditional financial systems and introduced new possibilities for wealth creation. This subsection explains the fundamental concepts of blockchain and explores its potential applications beyond cryptocurrencies. It delves into the benefits of decentralized ledgers, smart contracts, and tokenization in areas such as supply chain management, identity verification, and decentralized finance. It also discusses the risks and regulatory considerations associated with blockchain and cryptocurrencies.

3.5 Internet of Things (IoT): The Internet of Things (IoT) has connected physical devices and enabled the exchange of data on an unprecedented scale. This section explores how IoT is reshaping industries, from smart homes and cities to industrial automation and logistics. It discusses the opportunities presented by IoT, such as real-time data analytics, predictive maintenance, and enhanced customer experiences. It also addresses the challenges of data security, privacy, and interoperability in the IoT ecosystem.

3.6 Cloud Computing and Big Data: Cloud computing and big data technologies have revolutionized data storage, processing, and analytics. This subsection explores how cloud computing enables businesses to scale their operations, reduce infrastructure costs, and access advanced analytics capabilities. It discusses the power of big data in generating actionable insights, personalizing customer experiences, and driving innovation. It also addresses the ethical considerations and data privacy concerns associated with the collection and use of large-scale data.

3.7 Augmented and Virtual Reality: Augmented reality (AR) and virtual reality (VR) technologies have transformed the way we interact with digital content and immersive experiences. This section explores the applications of AR and VR in various industries, such as gaming, retail, real estate, and education. It discusses how these technologies enhance customer engagement, enable virtual simulations, and create new opportunities for marketing and product development.

3.8 Cybersecurity and Digital Trust: As wealth creation becomes increasingly reliant on digital technologies, cybersecurity and digital trust have become paramount. This subsection explores the challenges and risks associated with cybersecurity, including data breaches, ransomware attacks, and identity theft. It discusses the importance of building robust cybersecurity measures, fostering digital trust, and addressing the evolving threat landscape. It also examines emerging technologies, such as biometrics and encryption, that enhance security and protect digital assets.

Conclusion: Chapter 3 concludes by highlighting the transformative impact of revolutionary technologies on traditional wealth creation methods. It emphasizes the need for individuals and businesses to embrace these technologies to stay competitive, adapt to changing market dynamics, and seize new opportunities. By understanding and leveraging the power of automation, AI, blockchain, IoT, cloud computing, AR/VR, and cybersecurity, readers can position themselves to thrive in the evolving digital landscape and maximize their wealth creation potential.

CHAPTER 4: THE POWER OF DATA: HARNESSING ANALYTICS FOR PROFITABLE VENTURES

Introduction: Data has become a valuable asset in today's digital age, and harnessing its power through advanced analytics techniques is crucial for driving profitable ventures. This chapter explores the transformative potential of data analytics in unlocking valuable insights, making informed decisions, and optimizing business performance. By understanding and harnessing the power of data analytics, individuals and organizations can gain a competitive edge and capitalize on profitable opportunities.

4.1 The Data Revolution: The proliferation of digital technologies and interconnected systems has generated an unprecedented amount of data. This section introduces the concept of the data revolution and its impact on business operations and decision-making. It highlights the importance of data as a strategic asset and explores the challenges and opportunities associated with managing and leveraging vast data sets.

4.2 Foundations of Data Analytics: This subsection provides a foundation for understanding data analytics by explaining key concepts and techniques. It introduces descriptive, predictive, and prescriptive analytics and discusses their applications in various domains. It explores data preprocessing, data mining, statistical modeling, and machine learning algorithms as essential components of the analytics process. It also addresses the importance of data quality, data governance, and data ethics in ensuring reliable and ethical analytics outcomes.

4.3 Descriptive Analytics: Uncovering Insights from Historical Data: Descriptive analytics focuses on summarizing and visualizing historical data to gain insights into past events and trends. This section delves into exploratory data analysis, data visualization techniques, and statistical measures used to understand patterns, correlations, and distributions. It demonstrates how descriptive analytics can uncover valuable information about customer behavior, market trends, and operational performance, enabling businesses to make data-driven decisions.

4.4 Predictive Analytics: Forecasting and Anticipating Future Outcomes: Predictive analytics utilizes historical data and statistical modeling techniques to make predictions about future outcomes. This subsection explores regression analysis, time series forecasting, and predictive modeling algorithms. It discusses the application of predictive analytics in areas such as demand forecasting, customer segmentation, risk assessment, and fraud detection. It emphasizes the importance of selecting appropriate models and validating predictions to ensure their reliability.

4.5 Prescriptive Analytics: Optimizing Decisions and Actions: Prescriptive analytics goes beyond predicting outcomes by recommending optimal decisions and actions. This section introduces optimization techniques, simulation modeling, and decision support systems. It explains how prescriptive analytics can be applied to address complex business problems, such as resource allocation, supply chain optimization, pricing strategies, and investment portfolio management. It highlights the benefits of prescriptive analytics in improving efficiency, reducing costs, and maximizing profitability.

4.6 Big Data Analytics: Dealing with Volume, Velocity, and Variety: Big data analytics involves processing and analyzing massive volumes of data with high velocity and variety. This subsection explores technologies and tools, such as Hadoop, Spark, and NoSQL databases, that enable big data processing and storage. It discusses the challenges and opportunities associated with big data analytics, including data integration, data scalability, and real-time analytics. It also highlights the value of big data analytics in areas such as customer personalization, social media analysis, and Internet of Things (IoT) data insights.

4.7 Data-Driven Decision-Making: Data-driven decision-making is a paradigm that prioritizes evidence-based insights over intuition and gut feelings. This section emphasizes the importance of adopting a data-driven culture within organizations. It discusses the role of data governance, data literacy, and data-driven decision frameworks in enabling effective decision-making. It also explores the challenges of organizational change and the integration of data analytics into decision-making processes.

4.8 Ethical Considerations in Data Analytics: As data analytics becomes more prevalent, ethical considerations surrounding data privacy, security, and bias gain importance. This subsection addresses the ethical implications of data analytics and the need to prioritize privacy protection and transparency. It discusses regulatory frameworks, such as the General Data Protection Regulation (GDPR), and ethical guidelines for responsible data use. It emphasizes the importance of data ethics in maintaining trust and ensuring fair and unbiased analytics outcomes.

Conclusion: Chapter 4 concludes by highlighting the transformative power of data analytics in driving profitable ventures. It emphasizes the importance of leveraging descriptive, predictive, and prescriptive analytics techniques to gain insights, optimize decision-making, and improve business performance. By embracing data-driven decision-making, organizations can unlock the full potential of their data assets, gain a competitive advantage, and achieve profitable outcomes in today's data-driven business landscape.

CHAPTER 5: CRYPTO CRAZE: NAVIGATING THE WORLD OF DIGITAL ASSETS

Introduction: The rise of cryptocurrencies has created a global phenomenon, often referred to as the "crypto craze." This chapter explores the world of digital assets, providing insights into the concept of cryptocurrencies, their underlying technology, and the opportunities and challenges they present. By delving into the intricacies of the crypto landscape, readers can gain a deeper understanding of this evolving market and navigate it effectively.

5.1 Understanding Cryptocurrencies: This section provides an introduction to cryptocurrencies, explaining the concept of digital currencies that utilize cryptographic technology for secure transactions. It delves into the decentralized nature of cryptocurrencies, their independence from traditional financial institutions, and the role of blockchain technology in enabling transparent and tamper-proof transactions. It also addresses the significance of Bitcoin, the first and most well-known cryptocurrency, as well as the emergence of altcoins and stablecoins.

5.2 Blockchain Technology: Blockchain technology forms the foundation of cryptocurrencies, and understanding its mechanics is essential for navigating the crypto landscape. This subsection explores the core principles of blockchain, such as decentralized consensus, immutability, and smart contracts. It discusses the potential applications of blockchain beyond cryptocurrencies, including supply chain management, decentralized finance (DeFi), and identity verification. It also addresses the scalability and privacy challenges associated with blockchain technology.

5.3 Investment Opportunities: The crypto market offers a range of investment opportunities, but navigating this landscape requires careful consideration. This section explores the different investment options available, such as buying and holding cryptocurrencies, participating in initial coin offerings (ICOs), and engaging in crypto trading. It discusses the risks and rewards associated with each approach, highlights the importance of conducting thorough research, and emphasizes the need for risk management strategies in the highly volatile crypto market.

5.4 Crypto Exchanges and Wallets: Crypto exchanges serve as platforms for buying, selling, and trading cryptocurrencies. This subsection delves into the various types of exchanges, from centralized exchanges (CEXs) to decentralized exchanges (DEXs), and highlights their features, security measures, and regulatory considerations. It also discusses the importance of crypto wallets for securely storing and managing digital assets, exploring the different types of wallets, such as hardware wallets, software wallets, and online wallets.

5.5 Regulation and Legal Considerations: The

crypto landscape is evolving within a complex regulatory environment. This section examines the regulatory landscape for cryptocurrencies, discussing the approaches of different countries and jurisdictions. It explores the challenges associated with regulating digital assets, such as investor protection, anti-money laundering (AML) compliance, and taxation. It also addresses the need for individuals and businesses to understand and comply with applicable laws and regulations to ensure legal and secure participation in the crypto market.

5.6 Risks and Security: Cryptocurrencies are associated with unique risks and security considerations that investors must be aware of. This subsection discusses the risks of price volatility, market manipulation, and fraudulent schemes in the crypto market. It explores security best practices, such as securing private keys, implementing two-factor authentication (2FA), and conducting due diligence on projects and exchanges. It also provides insights into the importance of staying informed about security threats and adopting cybersecurity measures to protect digital assets.

5.7 Decentralized Finance (DeFi): Decentralized finance (DeFi) is an emerging sector within the crypto ecosystem that aims to recreate traditional financial services using blockchain technology. This section explores the concepts of DeFi, including decentralized lending, decentralized exchanges, and yield farming. It discusses the benefits and risks of participating in DeFi protocols, the challenges associated with auditing and security, and the potential impact of DeFi on traditional financial systems.

5.8 The Future of Cryptocurrencies: The crypto landscape is constantly evolving, and understanding the future prospects of cryptocurrencies is crucial. This subsection explores emerging trends and developments, such as central bank digital currencies (CBDCs), non-fungible tokens (NFTs), and scalability solutions. It discusses the potential impact of institutional adoption, regulatory developments, and technological advancements on the future of cryptocurrencies. It also emphasizes the need to stay informed and adapt to the changing dynamics of the crypto market.

Conclusion: Chapter 5 concludes by highlighting the importance of navigating the world of digital assets, particularly cryptocurrencies. It emphasizes the need for individuals and businesses to understand the fundamentals of cryptocurrencies, blockchain technology, and the associated investment opportunities and risks. By staying informed, conducting thorough research, adopting security measures, and complying with applicable regulations, readers can confidently navigate the crypto landscape and seize the potential benefits offered by this transformative market.

CHAPTER 6: THE FUTURE OF TRADING: THRIVING IN THE AGE OF HIGH-FREQUENCY TRADING

Introduction: The world of trading has undergone a significant transformation with the advent of high-frequency trading (HFT). This chapter explores the future of trading in the context of HFT, examining the impact of technology, algorithmic trading, and market structure changes. By understanding the dynamics of HFT and its implications, readers can gain insights into thriving in the evolving landscape of trading.

6.1 Understanding High-Frequency Trading: High-frequency trading involves the use of sophisticated algorithms and advanced technology to execute large volumes of trades at high speeds. This section provides an introduction to HFT, explaining its key features, such as low latency infrastructure, co-location, and algorithmic strategies. It discusses the motivations behind HFT, including profit generation, market liquidity provision, and risk management. It also addresses the criticisms and controversies associated with HFT, such as market manipulation concerns and potential systemic risks.

6.2 Technology and Infrastructure in HFT: Technology and infrastructure play a crucial role in enabling HFT. This subsection explores the technological advancements that support HFT, such as ultra-fast trading platforms, direct market access (DMA), and high-speed data feeds. It delves into the importance of low latency connectivity, hardware optimization, and proximity hosting in achieving competitive advantages. It also discusses the arms race for speed and the challenges faced by traders in maintaining cutting-edge technology.

6.3 Algorithmic Trading Strategies: Algorithmic trading lies at the core of HFT, allowing traders to execute trades based on pre-programmed rules and algorithms. This section examines popular algorithmic trading strategies used in HFT, such as market making, statistical arbitrage, and trend following. It discusses the quantitative models, technical indicators, and order execution algorithms employed in these strategies. It also highlights the role of machine learning and artificial intelligence in developing advanced algorithmic trading techniques.

6.4 Market Structure Changes: HFT has brought about significant changes in market structure, impacting the way trades are executed and market liquidity is provided. This subsection explores the evolution of market structure, including the rise of electronic trading platforms, dark pools, and alternative trading venues. It discusses the concept of fragmented markets and the challenges it poses for traders. It also addresses regulatory initiatives, such as MiFID II, aimed at promoting transparency and fairness in HFT-driven markets.

6.5 Risks and Challenges in HFT: HFT involves inherent

risks and challenges that traders must navigate. This section explores the risks associated with HFT, including market volatility, system glitches, and operational risks. It discusses the challenges of risk management in a high-speed trading environment and the importance of robust risk controls and monitoring systems. It also addresses the ethical considerations surrounding HFT, such as front-running and latency arbitrage, and the need for responsible trading practices.

6.6 The Role of Big Data and Artificial Intelligence: The increasing availability of big data and advancements in artificial intelligence (AI) have had a profound impact on HFT. This subsection explores the role of big data analytics and AI techniques, such as machine learning and natural language processing, in HFT. It discusses the use of big data for market analysis, sentiment analysis, and trade signal generation. It also examines the challenges and regulatory considerations associated with the use of AI in HFT.

6.7 Regulatory Landscape and Future Outlook: The rapid growth of HFT has prompted regulatory scrutiny and the implementation of measures to ensure market stability and fairness. This section explores the regulatory landscape governing HFT, discussing initiatives such as circuit breakers, market surveillance, and position limits. It also examines the future outlook of HFT, considering factors such as technological advancements, regulatory developments, and the potential impact of emerging technologies, such as blockchain and cryptocurrencies, on trading practices.

Conclusion: Chapter 6 concludes by emphasizing the need to adapt and thrive in the age of high-frequency trading. It highlights the importance of understanding the intricacies of HFT, including its technology, algorithmic strategies, market structure changes, and associated risks. By staying informed, embracing technological advancements, and implementing robust risk management practices, traders can position themselves to navigate the fast-paced world of HFT and capitalize on the opportunities presented by this evolving trading landscape.

CHAPTER 7: FROM TRADITIONAL TO DIGITAL: ADAPTING BUSINESS MODELS FOR SUCCESS

Introduction: In today's digital age, businesses are faced with the challenge of adapting to a rapidly changing landscape. This chapter explores the transition from traditional business models to digital business models, highlighting the opportunities and challenges it presents. By understanding the principles of digital transformation and embracing new approaches, businesses can position themselves for success in the digital era.

7.1 The Need for Digital Transformation: The rise of technology and changing consumer expectations have necessitated the need for digital transformation. This section examines the drivers behind digital transformation, including advancements in technology, evolving customer behaviors, and competitive pressures. It emphasizes the importance of embracing digital transformation to remain relevant, improve operational efficiency, and unlock new growth opportunities.

7.2 Understanding Digital Business Models: Digital business models differ significantly from traditional models, leveraging technology and data to create value and deliver superior customer experiences. This subsection explores the key components of digital business models, such as platform-based ecosystems, data-driven decision-making, and personalized customer interactions. It discusses the shift from product-centric to customer-centric approaches and the importance of agility and adaptability in digital business models.

7.3 Leveraging Technology for Competitive Advantage: Technology plays a pivotal role in digital business models, enabling businesses to gain a competitive edge. This section delves into the technological enablers of digital transformation, such as cloud computing, artificial intelligence, internet of things (IoT), and data analytics. It explores how businesses can leverage these technologies to enhance operational efficiency, optimize processes, and deliver innovative products and services.

7.4 Customer-Centricity and Personalization: Digital transformation places a strong emphasis on understanding and meeting customer needs. This subsection explores the importance of customer-centricity in digital business models. It discusses the use of data and analytics to gain insights into customer preferences, behavior, and journey. It also examines the role of personalization in delivering tailored experiences, building customer loyalty, and driving business growth.

7.5 Building Digital Ecosystems and Platforms: Digital transformation often involves the creation of digital ecosystems and platforms that facilitate collaboration, innovation, and value creation. This section delves into the concept of digital ecosystems, where multiple stakeholders collaborate to deliver integrated solutions. It discusses the benefits of ecosystem partnerships, open APIs, and co-creation. It also explores the platform business model, highlighting examples of successful platforms and the strategies for building and scaling digital platforms.

7.6 Agile and Lean Approaches: Digital transformation requires businesses to adopt agile and lean approaches to foster innovation, adaptability, and speed. This subsection explores agile methodologies, such as Scrum and Kanban, and their application in product development and project management. It discusses lean principles, focusing on eliminating waste, continuous improvement, and customer value creation. It emphasizes the importance of an agile and lean culture in driving successful digital transformation.

7.7 Reskilling and Talent Acquisition: Digital transformation necessitates a shift in skill sets and talent requirements. This section examines the importance of reskilling existing employees and acquiring new talent with digital capabilities. It discusses the need for a learning culture, upskilling programs, and attracting digital-native talent. It also explores the role of leadership in driving cultural change and fostering a digital mindset within the organization.

7.8 Overcoming Challenges and Risks: Digital transformation is not without its challenges and risks. This subsection addresses common challenges, such as legacy systems, resistance to change, and cybersecurity threats. It discusses strategies for managing these challenges, including legacy system modernization, change management processes, and cybersecurity measures. It also emphasizes the importance of risk management, compliance, and ethical considerations in the digital realm.

Conclusion: Chapter 7 concludes by highlighting the significance of adapting business models for success in the digital age. It underscores the need for businesses to embrace digital transformation, leveraging technology, customer-centricity, and agile approaches. By understanding the principles of digital business models and navigating the challenges and risks, businesses can position themselves for success and drive innovation, growth, and competitive advantage in the ever-evolving digital landscape.

CHAPTER 8: INVESTING IN INNOVATION: CAPITALIZING ON EMERGING INDUSTRIES

Introduction: Investing in emerging industries and innovative ventures has the potential to yield significant returns and drive economic growth. This chapter explores the concept of investing in innovation and capitalizing on emerging industries. It delves into the dynamics of identifying promising sectors, understanding disruptive technologies, and navigating the opportunities and challenges presented by investing in innovation.

8.1 The Rise of Emerging Industries: Emerging industries are characterized by the rapid development and adoption of new technologies, business models, and market trends. This section provides an overview of emerging industries, highlighting sectors such as renewable energy, biotechnology, artificial intelligence, blockchain, clean technologies, and space exploration. It discusses the factors driving their growth, including technological advancements, changing consumer preferences, and regulatory support.

8.2 Identifying Promising Sectors: Investing in emerging industries requires careful analysis and identification of promising sectors. This subsection explores strategies for identifying sectors with growth potential, such as market research, trend analysis, and analysis of macroeconomic factors. It discusses the importance of understanding market dynamics, competitive landscape, and regulatory environment. It also emphasizes the need for a long-term perspective and an understanding of industry-specific risks and challenges.

8.3 Understanding Disruptive Technologies: Emerging industries are often driven by disruptive technologies that reshape markets and create new opportunities. This section delves into key disruptive technologies, such as artificial intelligence, blockchain, Internet of Things, and gene editing. It explains their fundamental concepts, potential applications, and transformative impact on industries. It also discusses the investment opportunities and risks associated with investing in disruptive technologies.

8.4 Venture Capital and Startup Investing: Venture capital (VC) plays a crucial role in financing and supporting innovation-driven startups. This subsection explores the world of venture capital investing, discussing the process of identifying and evaluating startup opportunities, conducting due diligence, and structuring deals. It addresses the risks and rewards associated with venture capital investments, including high failure rates and potential for significant returns. It also highlights the importance of building a strong network and providing value-added support to portfolio companies.

8.5 Investing in Research and Development: Investing in research and development (R&D) is another avenue for capitalizing on innovation. This section explores the benefits of investing in R&D, such as intellectual property creation, technological advancements, and competitive advantage. It discusses the challenges of R&D investments, including long development cycles, high costs, and uncertain outcomes. It also examines strategies for managing R&D investments and leveraging collaborations with academic institutions and research organizations.

8.6 Social Impact Investing: Investing in emerging industries can go beyond financial returns and have a positive social and environmental impact. This subsection explores the concept of social impact investing, which aims to generate measurable social and environmental benefits alongside financial returns. It discusses impact investing strategies, such as sustainable investing, renewable energy investing, and social entrepreneurship. It highlights the importance of aligning investment goals with environmental, social, and governance (ESG) principles.

8.7 Global Opportunities and International Investments: Emerging industries offer global investment opportunities, as innovation is not limited to specific geographic regions. This section examines the benefits and challenges of international investments in emerging industries. It discusses factors to consider when investing internationally, such as political stability, regulatory frameworks, and cultural differences. It also explores strategies for diversifying investments geographically and leveraging global networks and partnerships.

8.8 Mitigating Risks and Challenges: Investing in emerging industries comes with its own set of risks and challenges. This subsection addresses the risks associated with investing in innovation, including technological uncertainties, market volatility, and regulatory changes. It discusses strategies for mitigating risks, such as conducting thorough due diligence, diversifying investments, and maintaining a long-term investment horizon. It also emphasizes the importance of continuously monitoring market trends and staying informed about industry developments.

Conclusion: Chapter 8 concludes by emphasizing the potential rewards of investing in innovation and emerging industries. It highlights the importance of identifying promising sectors, understanding disruptive technologies, and evaluating investment opportunities with a long-term perspective. By embracing the opportunities presented by emerging industries and employing effective risk management strategies, investors can position themselves to capitalize on innovation and drive financial returns while contributing to societal progress.

CHAPTER 9: DIVERSIFICATION DYNAMICS: BUILDING A RESILIENT AND LUCRATIVE PORTFOLIO

Introduction: Building a resilient and lucrative investment portfolio is a key objective for investors. This chapter explores the concept of diversification dynamics, emphasizing the importance of diversifying investments across different asset classes, geographies, and sectors. By understanding the dynamics of diversification, investors can mitigate risks, optimize returns, and create a resilient portfolio capable of withstanding market fluctuations.

9.1 The Power of Diversification: Diversification is a fundamental principle of investment management, aiming to reduce risk by spreading investments across different assets. This section explains the concept of diversification and its benefits. It discusses how diversification can help reduce portfolio volatility, preserve capital, and improve risk-adjusted returns. It also explores the relationship between risk and return and highlights the role of diversification in achieving a balance between the two.

9.2 Asset Class Diversification: Diversifying across different asset classes is a cornerstone of portfolio diversification. This subsection explores major asset classes, such as stocks, bonds, cash, real estate, and commodities. It discusses the characteristics and risk-return profiles of each asset class, highlighting their diversification potential. It also examines the role of alternative investments, such as private equity, hedge funds, and venture capital, in diversifying a portfolio beyond traditional asset classes.

9.3 Geographical Diversification: Geographical diversification involves investing in different regions and countries to reduce exposure to country-specific risks and capture global growth opportunities. This section explores the benefits of geographical diversification, including reduced political and economic risks, exposure to diverse market cycles, and access to emerging markets. It discusses considerations when diversifying geographically, such as currency risk, regulatory differences, and cultural nuances.

9.4 Sector and Industry Diversification: Sector and industry diversification involves allocating investments across different sectors of the economy to reduce exposure to specific industry risks. This subsection delves into the benefits of sector diversification, including improved risk management, exposure to various growth sectors, and potential for outperformance. It discusses strategies for sector diversification, such as analyzing industry trends, assessing sector correlations, and aligning investment themes with long-term economic shifts.

9.5 Time Horizon and Diversification: Time horizon plays a crucial role in diversification dynamics. This section explores the relationship between time horizon and diversification strategies. It discusses the impact of time horizon on investment goals, risk tolerance, and asset allocation decisions. It emphasizes the need to align diversification strategies with investment horizons, considering factors such as liquidity requirements, investment objectives, and time-sensitive investment opportunities.

9.6 Rebalancing and Portfolio Monitoring: Maintaining an effective diversification strategy requires regular portfolio monitoring and rebalancing. This subsection explores the importance of monitoring portfolio performance, asset allocation, and risk exposure. It discusses the triggers for portfolio rebalancing, such as deviations from target asset allocation, changing market conditions, and shifting investment objectives. It also addresses the challenges and considerations of portfolio rebalancing, including transaction costs and tax implications.

9.7 Diversification and Risk Management: Diversification is closely linked to risk management. This section explores the role of diversification in mitigating different types of risks, such as market risk, credit risk, and geopolitical risk. It discusses strategies for risk management through diversification, including the use of low-correlated assets, hedging techniques, and risk assessment models. It also examines the limitations of diversification and the importance of comprehensive risk management strategies.

9.8 Dynamic Diversification Strategies: Diversification

is not a static concept; it requires ongoing adjustments based on market conditions and investor objectives. This subsection explores dynamic diversification strategies, such as tactical asset allocation and factor-based investing. It discusses the benefits of dynamically adjusting asset allocations based on market trends, valuations, and economic indicators. It also explores the use of factors, such as value, momentum, and quality, in constructing diversified portfolios that align with specific investment objectives.

9.9 Behavioral Considerations in Diversification: Investor behavior plays a significant role in the success of diversification strategies. This section explores behavioral considerations in diversification, such as herding behavior, overconfidence, and loss aversion. It discusses the impact of behavioral biases on investment decisions and the importance of discipline, patience, and rational decision-making in implementing effective diversification strategies. It also explores techniques for overcoming behavioral biases and improving diversification outcomes.

Conclusion: Chapter 9 concludes by highlighting the importance of diversification dynamics in building a resilient and lucrative portfolio. It emphasizes the need to diversify across asset classes, geographies, and sectors to mitigate risks and optimize returns. By understanding the power of diversification, regularly monitoring and rebalancing portfolios, and considering behavioral aspects, investors can create a resilient portfolio capable of withstanding market uncertainties and capturing long-term growth opportunities.

CHAPTER 10: SUSTAINABLE SUCCESS: BALANCING PROFITABILITY AND ETHICAL PRACTICES

Introduction: In today's business landscape, the pursuit of sustainable success goes beyond financial profitability. This chapter explores the concept of balancing profitability with ethical practices, emphasizing the importance of incorporating social and environmental considerations into business strategies. By understanding the dynamics of sustainable business practices, organizations can create long-term value while addressing societal and environmental challenges.

10.1 The Rise of Sustainability: Sustainability has gained prominence as organizations recognize the need to balance profit generation with social and environmental responsibility. This section explores the evolution of sustainability as a business imperative. It discusses the emergence of sustainability frameworks, such as the triple bottom line (people, planet, profit) and the United Nations Sustainable Development Goals (SDGs). It also examines the benefits of sustainable practices, including enhanced brand reputation, stakeholder engagement, and risk management.

10.2 Defining Ethical Practices: Ethical practices encompass behaviors and actions that align with moral principles and societal values. This subsection delves into the concept of ethical practices, exploring ethical frameworks and standards, such as corporate social responsibility (CSR) and business ethics. It discusses the importance of ethical decision-making, transparency, and accountability in building trust with stakeholders. It also examines the relationship between ethics and sustainable business practices.

10.3 Integrating Sustainability into Business Strategies: Integrating sustainability into business strategies involves embedding social and environmental considerations throughout the organization's operations and decision-making processes. This section explores strategies for incorporating sustainability into business models, including sustainable supply chain management, responsible sourcing, and product life cycle assessment. It also discusses the role of sustainability metrics, reporting frameworks, and impact assessments in driving organizational change.

10.4 Corporate Social Responsibility (CSR): Corporate Social Responsibility (CSR) is an approach that encourages businesses to consider the impact of their activities on society and the environment. This subsection examines the concept of CSR, including philanthropy, employee volunteering, and community engagement. It explores the benefits of CSR, such as enhanced brand reputation, employee satisfaction, and customer loyalty. It also discusses the role of CSR in addressing social and environmental challenges, such as income inequality and climate change.

10.5 Environmental Sustainability: Environmental sustainability focuses on minimizing negative environmental impacts and promoting the responsible use of natural resources. This section explores strategies for achieving environmental sustainability, such as adopting renewable energy sources, reducing carbon emissions, and implementing waste reduction and recycling programs. It discusses the benefits of environmental sustainability, including cost savings, regulatory compliance, and resilience to climate-related risks.

10.6 Social Impact and Stakeholder Engagement: Social impact involves creating positive changes in society through business practices. This subsection explores strategies for generating social impact, such as promoting diversity and inclusion, supporting local communities, and fostering ethical labor practices. It discusses the importance of stakeholder engagement, including employees, customers, communities, and investors, in driving social impact and building sustainable relationships.

10.7 Ethical Leadership and Governance: Ethical leadership and governance are critical for establishing a culture of ethical practices within organizations. This section examines the role of leaders in promoting ethical behavior, setting the tone from the top, and creating an ethical organizational culture. It discusses the importance of governance structures, ethics codes, and whistleblower mechanisms in ensuring accountability and transparency. It also explores the relationship between ethical leadership, sustainable practices, and long-term business success.

10.8 Responsible Investing: Responsible investing integrates environmental, social, and governance (ESG) factors into investment decision-making. This subsection explores the concept of responsible investing, including impact investing, socially responsible investing (SRI), and ESG integration. It discusses the growing demand for responsible investment options, the role of ESG ratings and benchmarks, and the potential financial benefits of incorporating sustainability considerations into investment strategies.

10.9 Collaboration and Partnerships for Sustainable Success: Achieving sustainable success often requires collaboration and partnerships with stakeholders across sectors. This section explores the importance of collaboration, including public-private partnerships, industry coalitions, and cross-sector initiatives. It discusses the benefits of collective action in addressing complex social and environmental challenges and driving systemic change. It also examines the role of innovation and technology in fostering collaborative solutions.

Conclusion: Chapter 10 concludes by highlighting the importance of balancing profitability with ethical practices for sustainable success. It emphasizes the need for organizations to integrate sustainability into their strategies, foster ethical leadership, and engage stakeholders in driving positive social and environmental impacts. By embracing ethical practices, organizations can enhance their brand reputation, attract and retain talent, and contribute to a more sustainable and equitable future for society and the planet.